Creating Diversity-Rich Environments for Young Children

Other Redleaf Press Books by Angèle Sancho Passe

Dual-Language Learners: Strategies for Teaching English

Is Everybody Ready for Kindergarten?: A Tool Kit for Preparing Children and Families

Evaluating and Supporting Early Childhood Teachers

Redleaf *Quick* Guide

Creating Diversity-Rich Environments for Young Children

Angèle Sancho Passe

Redleaf Press®
www.redleafpress.org
800-423-8309

Published by Redleaf Press
10 Yorkton Court
St. Paul, MN 55117
www.redleafpress.org

First edition 2020
Senior editor: Melissa York
Managing editor: Douglas Schmitz
Cover design: Jim Handrigan
Cover photo: © iStock.com/FatCamera
Typeset in Signo and Avenir by Douglas Schmitz
Printed in the United States of America

Library of Congress Cataloging-in-Publication Data

Names: Passe, Angèle Sancho, author.
Title: Creating diversity-rich environments for young children / Angèle
   Sancho Passe.
Description: First edition. | St. Paul, MN : Redleaf Press, 2020. |
   Includes bibliographical references. | Summary: "Creating Diversity-Rich
   Environments for Young Children focuses on how early childhood
   professionals can create a positive and inclusive environment for
   children of all cultures"— Provided by publisher.
Identifiers: LCCN 2020008055 (print) | LCCN 2020008056 (ebook) | ISBN
   9781605546650 (paperback) | ISBN 9781605546667 (ebook)
Subjects: LCSH: Early childhood education--United States. | Multicultural
   education--United States. | Classroom environment--United States.
Classification: LCC LB1139.25 .P375 2020 (print) | LCC LB1139.25 (ebook)
   | DDC 372.210973--dc23
LC record available at https://lccn.loc.gov/2020008055
LC ebook record available at https://lccn.loc.gov/2020008056

Printed on acid-free paper   U24-05

To all early educators striving to create
diversity-rich environments for young children

CONTENTS

CONTENTS

INTRODUCTION

Multicultural, cross-cultural, intercultural, or *diversity-rich*? Terms change and evolve. It is challenging to find one unique word that fits everybody's vision. For some thinkers, *multicultural* refers to a society that has several cultural or ethnic groups. Even though people live next to each other, they do not necessarily interact deeply with each other. They may enjoy each other's restaurants but not exchange ideas. For other thinkers, *cross-cultural* has more to do with the comparison of different cultures. Many cultures are compared to one another and to one dominant culture. In a cross-cultural mindset, people understand each other but they are not transformed. In more recent thinking, *intercultural* reflects the idea of a search for deeper understanding and respect for all cultures. In an intercultural society, everyone feels a positive impact because everyone learns from one another and grows together. *Diversity-rich* means understanding that everyone is unique and recognizing individual differences. It requires conscious practice of mutual respect, sharing each other's cultures.

In this book, we will use the term *diversity-rich* to acknowledge that our early childhood environments have a vast variety of cultures in the children, families, and staff members. We will also make reference to the term *equity*, as presented in the recently published position statement from the National Association for the Education of Young Children (NAEYC): Advancing Equity in Early Childhood Education (NAEYC 2019). It is not enough to embrace diversity. The lens must be sharpened to include fairness and justice in our work with children, families, and colleagues.

To help you keep your focus on equity, a box at the beginning of each chapter correlates the material to specific recommendations of the NAEYC position statement on Advancing Equity in Early Childhood Education. The recommendations in the position statement are divided into several categories: Recommendations for Everyone; Recommendations for Early Childhood Educators; Recommendations for Administrators of Schools, Centers, Family Child Care Homes, and Other Early Childhood Education Settings; Recommendations for those Facilitating Educator Preparation and Professional Development; and Recommendations for Public

Policymakers. The Advancing Equity position statement is available at www.naeyc.org/resources/position-statements/equity. You can scan the QR code to the right to go straight to the statement.

The objectives of this book are the following:

- To examine what a diversity-rich environment looks like and why it is important in early childhood education.

- To recognize the expertise you already have, so you increase your confidence.

- To present practical strategies to use with children, families, and colleagues.

- To help you make a personal plan that you can follow as you continue to grow in your skills.

The word *skill* is important. The topic of diversity is loaded with emotion. In reality, this is the first time in history that big numbers of people of so many diverse cultures must interact with each other peacefully. It is the first time that the law mandates us all to get along and collaborate in a variety of settings, from schools to offices to churches and from private to public places. In a global mindset of welcoming many cultures, we must be conscious of the weight of the endeavor. The emotion must be self-regulated. The wise mind must prevail.

Definition of Culture

Culture is about the daily experiences that shape people's understanding of life. It is the activities, memories, and language we share. Daily experiences for young children include how babies are comforted, the way they are cuddled, how and what they are fed, and where they sleep. For older children, it means the games they play, the books they are read, and the number of toys they have.

Dimensions of Culture

Cultural identity is complex. It is more than ethnicity, language, or skin color. There is not just one way that we think of ourselves. Many aspects describe who we are, like gender, nationality, race, ethnicity, age, language, family background, religion, home/geographic roots, socioeconomic status, physical ability, mental ability, sexual orientation, work experience, and educational background. The list is long. Below are examples to help you ponder the many dimensions your children experience. These dimensions also apply to the families and to the staff members who work with the children and families.

Children may have direct experience with all these dimensions of diversity at home or in your program. They may also have more distant interactions in their neighborhood or community.

Age includes the stages of life from infants to the elderly in the same family. As life expectancy increases, young children now have two generations of elders in their family: great-grandparents and others of the same generation, as well as grandparents, grand-aunts, and granduncles. They may have elderly neighbors or interact with elderly volunteers while in a child care setting. Some may be using canes or wheelchairs. Children may also have younger or older siblings.

Education can be formal and informal. Families have varied levels of formal education and training. That affects children's levels of language development and early literacy. For example, children in households with high literacy are likely to have more opportunities for reading and a more developed vocabulary.

Ethnicity includes factors such as nationality, regional culture, ancestry, religion, and language in addition to race.

Family constellation describes varying family size and configuration. Children may live in a single parent or two-parent nuclear family with parents and children living together. Increasingly families are becoming more permeable and fluid with stepchildren, stepparents, and other older or younger relatives. Pets may be important family members too.

Gender is a social concept that defines the attitudes, behaviors, and roles that a society or culture associates traditionally with an individual's sex, such as female and male; current social science is challenging this notion to view gender as fluid. Children or family members may identify with genders such as nonbinary or transgender.

Home/geographic roots is where children live. It may be in the community where they and their parents were born. Others may have moved within the country for practical reasons such as employment or schooling. Other children are immigrants or refugees who come from faraway lands with different customs and languages.

Language is human speech and written expression. Some children are monolingual English speakers, while others are dual-language learners, speaking English and a home language. Some children may even have more than one home language. Exposure to languages may be written or oral. Parents may have varied fluency and literacy levels in the languages of their family.

Mental ability shapes the experiences of people in diverse ways. A condition may affect the ability of the brain to read, think, or make decisions. It may be caused by mental illness, brain injury, or addiction. Children may have a condition that affects their mental ability or know other children or adults who do.

Nationality is the condition of belonging to a particular nation. New immigrants in a country belong to the nationality of their home country. They may be from Somalia or France and live in the United States as permanent residents.

Neurodiversity is the idea that neurological differences are to be recognized and respected like any other human variation. Conditions such as autism spectrum or dyslexia are the result of variations in the human genome. Therefore, acceptance and accommodations help everyone feel respected and productive.

Occupation is the type of work that parents do and where they work. Occupation is usually related to the socioeconomic status of children.

Physical ability shapes the experiences of people in diverse ways. This depends on general health (breathing, mobility, hearing, sight, strength). Children may have a condition from birth or due to an illness or injury that affects the abilities of their body, or they may know other children or adults with such conditions.

Race is a social construct under which people of the same race share certain physical characteristics (skin color, eye color, bone structure, hair). The Census Bureau defines race as "a person's self-identification with one or more social groups. An individual can report as White, Black or African American, Asian, American Indian and Alaska Native, Native Hawaiian and Other Pacific Islander, or some other race. Survey respondents may report multiple races." Note that the concept of race is confusing and controversial. It is mostly a bureaucratic definition in the United States. Race and ethnicity data are used primarily to make funding decisions for education, employment, or health.

Religion is a belief in God or gods. The US Constitution guarantees freedom of religion. Many children live in households who follow a religion. If they do not, they may be atheist or agnostic. The church or temple community is important to many families and a place to gather with others who have the same beliefs.

Sexual orientation describes a person's pattern of attraction—emotional, romantic, sexual, or some combination of these—to another sex, the same sex, multiple sexes, or none. Families may be headed by lesbian, gay, bisexual, or heterosexual individuals or couples or by people who fall elsewhere on that spectrum.

Socioeconomic status impacts the daily experiences of children according to the income levels of their families. Affluence and poverty affect families' access to materials, food, and activities.

Reasons for Optimism

Despite media alarms about lack of respect for diversity, there is reason for optimism. Never before have so many people paid attention to the topic. It is the right time to give practical solutions to early educators so they feel more confident and are more competent in teaching all children well. In an increasingly global atmosphere, cultural issues must be addressed in a matter-of-fact and direct way. You have an important and difficult job. This book offers to make creating diversity-rich environments manageable.

CHAPTER 1:
FRAMEWORKS FOR CREATING
A DIVERSITY-RICH ENVIRONMENT

Advancing Equity in Early Childhood Education (NAEYC 2019)

Recommendations for Everyone: 1, 2, 3, 4, 5, 6

Diversity is all dimensions of culture interacting with each other. We see it in our classrooms with children, families, and colleagues. We see diversity in our own families too. Take the time to think about your classroom and your program. Reflect on the children, families, and colleagues. Write their names in a column and note how they illustrate the list of cultural dimensions you have just read.

Recognizing diversity is seeing the many ways that people understand daily life. Having a diversity-rich perspective as an early childhood educator is being interested in what families do at home with their children. *Having an open mind* does not mean accepting everything families do as good. *Respecting many ways of understanding daily life* does not mean ignoring what's important for children. For example, research says reading is good for children because it increases their vocabulary, and vocabulary is a measure of reading success. If families do not read to children at home, early educators know it is not best practice. However, they should not blame families. Their job is to explain to families why reading is good for children—and make sure to read extra books to children in their program.

Educators often express concerns about their work with diversity: "I don't know about other cultures," "I only speak English," "I am uncomfortable with the idea of LGBTQ," "I didn't grow up with people of different races." We can never know everything there is to know about other people, so we acknowledge that there is not a magic formula. As you learn more about creating diversity-rich environments, you might be worried about how to do it well. You might be afraid of making mistakes. You might not feel simple neutral acceptance of others. But it is a skill that must be learned and worked at. The result is the immense satisfaction of doing a good job.

A big point of honoring diversity is to add to what families do at home and give them ideas and skills to help them feel confident and competent. Families want their children to succeed in the world in which they live. They have high hopes that their children will be able to be good learners, workers, and productive members of society. Children do not just live in the cultural bubble of their families. They also live in the outside world of school and community.

How Children Experience Diversity

Between ages two and five, children develop their sense of self. They become aware of the gender, culture, ethnicity, family differences, disabilities, and economic class of themselves and others. In the presence of people who are different from them, they may say things like "Why is he Black?" "She looks funny." "Why doesn't she walk?" "I don't like him, he is weird." "Boys can't play here." "Girls are weak." "You can't have two mommies!" "Muslims are stupid." These questions and comments are an expression of curiosity or discomfort. The children may be repeating things they have heard others say.

At the same time, young children become aware of biases against aspects of their own identity. With adult guidance, preschoolers can begin to recognize and challenge biases, unfairness, racism, and sexism that affect themselves and others. This is even more reason for creating diversity-rich environments for all children. We want children to develop a strong self-concept. We also want them to respect and interact in positive ways with people who are different from themselves.

Understanding Bias and Discrimination

Bias is an attitude, belief, or feeling that results in and helps justify unfair treatment of a person because of her or his identity. For example, there is evidence that early childhood teachers believe that young Black boys need to be watched more closely than other children (Gilliam et al. 2016), lest they cause trouble in the classroom. That is a bias.

Discrimination is an action by an institution or individual that denies access or opportunity to people based on some aspect of their identity (such as gender, income, or race). Discrimination is regulated by strict laws in the United States. In the case of the Black boys, it means that their access to early childhood programs is open. There is no legal discrimination against them. However, because of the bias described above, these children are targeted for expulsion from programs at rates two to three times higher than other children (Brown and Steele 2015). According to data from the Office of Civil Rights (OCR), Black children make up 18 percent of preschool enrollment but 48 percent of preschool children receiving suspension (OCR 2014).

Therefore, even though they have access to education, they are denied the opportunity to learn. The implicit bias of educators affects their experience in a negative way.

Children are at risk of being harmed by the biases of educators in other ways too. Other examples include ignoring the languages of immigrant children; high child-adult ratios that make quality care impossible; being friendlier to children from one culture than another; the persistent education gap between children of color and white children; not providing enough physical activities; ignoring that children live in gay and lesbian families; and using classroom management techniques that are harsher for some children than others. But in all of these examples, there is hope. When educators become aware of their biases, they are more intentional in delivering good education to all children.

Useful Resources and Philosophies

There is a solid body of research and ideas to help educators do a good job with cultural diversity. Every state has developed Early Learning Standards to understand early childhood development. Institutions like the National Association for the Education of Young Children (NAEYC) and the National Black Child Development Institute (NBCDI) provide information and resources. Concepts like cultural pluralism, anti-bias education, cultural guidance, and skilled dialogue are important tools.

An Environment That Helps Black Children Learn

Debra Ren-Etta Sullivan (2016), the author of *Cultivating the Genius of Black Children*, proposes twelve key elements of the learning environment that will best help Black children learn:

1. Active, engaged, synergetic learning

2. Interactive discourse, discussion, and analysis with an emphasis on verbal "play"

3. Opportunities for creativity, individualism, and embellishment

4. Collective/collaborative activity and problem solving

5. Competitive mental and physical challenges

6. Meaningful, mutually respectful teacher-child relationship

7. Meaningful, mutually respectful connection to family and community

8. Educational empowerment/personal responsibility

9. Opportunities for self-reflection

10. Opportunities for connecting with nature and each other for a higher purpose or a good cause

11. An integrated, connected curriculum

12. A sense of community and belonging (p. 75–76)

Reading this list, you might notice that they are the same expectations promoted by early childhood education environmental assessments like the CLASS, the ELLCO, or the ECERS. They are the same as the principles of Developmentally Appropriate Practice (NAEYC) and many other works that describe quality early childhood education. Many children benefit from these positive teachings, but unfortunately these ideas are less often applied when teaching Black children. When these children are creative, interactive, or physical, their behaviors are likely to be interpreted in a negative way by their teachers. The teachers hold the bias that these children do not have the inherent abilities to do well without stricter direction. They work to curb the creativity, interaction, and physicality by insisting on quiet and passive behaviors. In turn, these unfair requests generate resistance from the children, resulting in a negative cycle. The solution is that all these ideas must be applied for all children, regardless of race. And it must happen all day, every day.

Early Learning Standards

The Early Learning Standards guide educators in understanding child development and design curriculum and activities that best meet the needs of children. Every state has Early Learning Standards as a tool for knowing how children grow in different areas of development: social-emotional, physical, and cognitive skills; language and literacy; arts; and approaches to learning. Before the age of three, children learn about themselves. Then they begin to know about others.

NAEYC Code of Ethical Conduct and Developmentally Appropriate Practices

As a field, we have the guidance of NAEYC, which gives a clear path for doing the right things for children, families, and colleagues in the Code of Ethical Conduct and in the Developmentally Appropriate Practices Model. As the NAEYC Code of Ethical Conduct (2011) states:

> We shall not participate in practices that discriminate against children by denying benefits, giving special advantages, or excluding them from programs or activities on the basis of their sex, race, national origin, immigration status, preferred home language, religious belief, medical condition, disability, or the marital status/family structure, sexual orientation, or religious beliefs or other affiliations of their families. (p. 3)

Most importantly, the first item in the NAEYC Code of Ethical Conduct states:

> We shall not harm children. We shall not participate in practices that are emotionally damaging, physically harmful, disrespectful, degrading, dangerous, exploitative, or intimidating to children. (2011, 3)

Early educators must reflect on the "harm" aspect of bias, which results in not teaching all children with fairness. It harms children when the following occurs:

- They hear their home language only when the teacher scolds them.

- They are picked last to go to lunch because they were the wiggliest at circle time.

- Expectations are lower because their family is below the poverty line.

- They have two fathers and there are no books about families with two dads on the bookshelf.

- The teacher ignores the multicultural richness of their classroom.

Cultural Pluralism

Janet Gonzalez-Mena describes cultural pluralism as "the notion that groups and individuals should be allowed, even encouraged, to hold on to what gives them their unique identities, while maintaining their membership in the larger social framework." She adds, "The goal of diversity is unity. Only when we can come together freely, as we are, feeling good about who we are, can we create a healthy unity among all the people of this great society" (2008, 14).

Cultural pluralism

- gives guidance in planning curriculum;

- gives guidance in designing the environment;

- relates to the Early Learning Standard of Self and Emotional Awareness;

- relates to the Early Learning Standard of Building Relationships; and

- gives guidance in choosing books for the library center.

Anti-Bias Education

Anti-bias education was pioneered in the early childhood setting by Louise Derman-Sparks and her colleagues (Derman-Sparks et al. 2009; Derman-Sparks et al. 2015; Derman-Sparks et al. 2011). Children are aware of differences in themselves and others at a very young age, and anti-bias education is a positive way to teach about diversity. Young children are also capable of addressing unfairness at their level of development. They can find solutions when educators and parents teach them how to do it. For example, in one classroom, children examined books on the shelf and discussed if the families in the books looked like theirs. Over the course of one month of study, they determined that there were no books with Asian characters (there were two Asian children in the group) and no books with families with two moms (there was one such family in the group). Based on their investigation, they wrote a request to the director to buy books that reflected their classroom community. In addition, the program added to the curriculum a family activity night during which they made books with pictures of all the children and their families for the classroom.

Anti-bias education

- becomes a practice for choosing learning and teaching materials;

- addresses the experiences of monocultural groups of children;

- helps children learn the difference between feelings of superiority and feelings of self-esteem surrounding their heritage;

- gives tools to talk openly about the various family structures of children in the classroom; and

- helps address the stereotypical beliefs that parents or guardians who are low income are not good parents.

Cultural Guidance

Lisa Delpit (2006) advanced the notion that some members of society do not have inside knowledge about how to access the culture of power. This may be the case for families of color, immigrants, or people with low education. Even at the early childhood level, the jargon of our field is complicated for parents to understand. While it may be clear to us, they may not know the path to kindergarten. In that case, Delpit says that educators need to be "cultural guides." She makes the distinction between being a cultural guide rather than being a cultural invader. A cultural invader says, *your language and culture are wrong. If you want to be successful, you need to adopt the dominant culture and forget yours.* Educators may deliver this message with or without words by failing to acknowledge home cultures. A cultural guide, on the other hand says, *your language and culture are valuable. They are part of who you are. I will help you keep them up. At the same time, I will show you how things are done here so you learn the rules and ways of contemporary American culture.* The cultural guide acknowledges home cultures and understands deeply that all families share the universal values of love, protection, and nurturance. A cultural guide knows that these values are expressed and lived differently. Guides also understand that such differences may need to be discussed and navigated with diplomacy and compassion.

Cultural guidance

- respects the confidence of teachers in their own skills;

- allows teachers to give parents information about the field of early education in a respectful way;

- encourages parents to choose how they want to acculturate; and

- teaches children how to adjust to the rules and demands of life in child care or school, which may be different from home.

Skilled Dialogue

Isaura Barrera developed the model of skilled dialogue (Barrera and Corso 2003; Barrera and Kramer 2017). It is an approach that honors cultural beliefs and values. Educators value the earlier experiences of children and families and use them as the foundation for learning new ways. In a reciprocal relationship, educators tune in to families' hopes, dreams, and definition of success for their children. They listen more and find ways to collaborate successfully.

Skilled dialogue

- encourages educators to develop a relationship with families based on common goals for children;

- asks educators to suspend judgement;

- promotes respectful and responsive interactions;

- reframes differences between educators and families as complementary rather than contradictory.

Personal and Professional Experience of Educators

Educators often ignore their own personal and professional experiences as part of the cultural community of their classroom or program. In my work as trainer and coach, I hear educators, especially white educators, claim they don't have a culture. Yet your culture is important too. As you acknowledge your own culture and add it to the culture of children, you create a diverse community where everyone appreciates one another. You also know a lot about child development and teaching. You have characteristics that predispose you to be good at creating a positive, diversity-rich environment. More information may be necessary to make you more aware and to go deeper, but your foundation is strong.

It's important for you to remember and acknowledge that

- you are a good person who cares about children;

- you have studied early childhood development;

- you attend conferences and professional development workshops to enhance your knowledge;

- you are skilled at teaching young children; and

- your culture is part of the diversity in your classroom or program.

CHAPTER 2:
VALUES AND ATTITUDES

Advancing Equity in Early Childhood Education (NAEYC 2019)

Recommendations for Everyone: 1, 2, 3, 4, 5, 6

Recommendations for Early Childhood Educators:

- Create a Caring, Equitable Community of Engaged Learners: 1, 2, 4, 5, 6, 8, 9, 10

- Establish Reciprocal Relationships with Families: 1, 2, 3, 4, 5

- Observe, Document, and Assess Children's Learning and Development: 1, 2, 3

In a child care center, an immigrant father asked that his son not play in the housekeeping center of his classroom. He worried that his little boy would learn behavior inappropriate for a male of his culture. The teacher, a man, listened to the father carefully. He knew about the practice of skilled dialogue, where the objective is to consider the family's view and the educator's view and combine both to arrive at a solution. The teacher explained to the father that, in his classroom, he follows the philosophy of developmentally appropriate practice and that all the children must have access to all the materials and spaces in the room. He stated that while he heard the concerns of the father, he could not deny access to the housekeeping area to the boy or to any other child. The father and the teacher had several conversations about the choices each could make at home and at school. They concluded that the family could control play at home, but school was a diverse, developmentally appropriate learning environment, and therefore the child had the right to play everywhere in the classroom. The father decided that he would not let his son "play kitchen" at home, but he wanted the child to continue his American education at school with the same teacher.

Examining Values and Attitudes in a Diversity-Rich Environment

Early education is all about relationships. Working with children also means working with their families. And of course, it means working with colleagues. All that occurs in very intimate ways. We hear details about children's family life every day. Families ask for our advice, but they do not always take it. Educators feel frustrated because their view of the world does not always jibe with the reality of children's lives.

Values are a person's principles or standards of behaviors. These standards are often shared with a cultural group, but they may also be an individual's judgement of what's important in life. That means that there are many values, with many variations.

Attitude is a settled way of feeling or thinking about someone or something. It is often shown with behavior. Therefore, one could say that our attitudes are an expression or consolidation of our values. If I hold the value that children learn though play, and I hold the value that children must learn the alphabet before kindergarten, I will teach the alphabet with songs and engaging activities rather than rote repetition. I will do so intentionally. This intentionality is my attitude.

Important Considerations for Educators

Be Aware, Be Alert, Be Intentional

The first part of examining our values and attitudes is to be aware of our biases. Everyone has biases, and we must always bring them to our consciousness so we don't blindly act on them. The consequences of ignoring our biases are always negative.

Believe That Families Want the Best for Their Children

Depending on their level of education and knowledge, families have diverse ways of viewing early childhood education. Highly educated families tend to do a lot of research to choose the program that best fits their needs. These parents feel confident in their ability to advocate for their child, so they ask about the curriculum or teacher turnover. Immigrant families, families in poverty, and families with low educational levels are less familiar with the culture of education. They are not as aware of their choices, and they may not know how to conduct the search. They expect that educators will provide the best for their children. Even though they may have different traditions and practices, all families want their children to succeed.

Embrace the Concept of Universal Family Values

No family wants their child to be sad, sick, poorly adjusted, or unready for school. Protecting, educating, and nurturing children are universal core values of the family. Throughout the world, all families want children to become productive adults in their own culture. In a diverse society, knowing the "code for success" is difficult. It may have been simpler in the past when there were fewer life choices and when people lived in smaller communities or groups. Educators with a diversity-rich mindset must embrace this idea of universal core values. That belief enables us to support families even when we disagree with their practices.

Know That Values Are Demonstrated through Practices and Traditions

Families have ways of doing things that may be part of the larger culture or may be specific to their small unit. This happens in how they celebrate cultural or religious holidays like Christmas or the Fourth of July or private holidays like birthdays or graduations. Families also have their own daily routines such as mealtime and bedtime. They handle illness, vacations, gatherings, and prayers in thousands of different manners. Sometimes they make pragmatic decisions. For example, Muslim Somali families in the United States may take part in the Christmas gift giveaways. In this case, parents see the benefit to their children of getting new toys, independent of religious beliefs.

Be Curious about Other Peoples' Values and Practices

As early educators, we get a glimpse into the children's lives when they or their parents tell us stories. We may be surprised by what we hear. Curiosity is a healthy attitude. Not in a judgmental way, but in an open way that celebrates the richness of expression for those universal values of protection, education, and nurturance. We also want to remember that values and practices or traditions may change with new experiences. It is always possible to add or drop some. This may start with concrete experiences such as a potluck at your child care program where families share their favorite dishes. And it may go deeper, as when a teacher honors the many languages of the children in her classroom by learning fingerplays in each of the languages to routinely integrate them into her lesson plans.

Children Must Learn the Skills to Be Successful in the Country Where They Live

For a school district, I conducted focus groups to find out what parents wanted for their children's education. The goal was to get information from a wide variety of families. The groups had different socioeconomic, language, ethnic, and educational characteristics. They were American-born white people and people of color, immigrants, refugees, teen parents, and older parents. To the question, "What do you want for your children when they grow up?" all answered that they wanted their children to succeed in life and at work in the United States. The more affluent and educated families had a map of the path to their vision of success, including the education needed and the desired livelihoods their children might pursue. The less affluent, the less educated, and the immigrants had the same vision of success, but they did not know the path. That is an important concept for educators to remember. It is tempting to jump to the conclusion that some families do not value education when they don't attend parent-teacher conferences. This assumption is a dangerous bias. It lowers our respect for families. It diminishes our ability to teach the children the skills they need to succeed.

Practical Applications

Strategies for Creating a Diversity-Rich Environment with an Equity Lens

- **Be aware of your personal values and professional responsibilities.** Personal values and professional responsibilities may sometimes be in conflict. In a professional situation, your professional responsibilities as an educator come first. Early educators must follow best practices in early childhood education, and they must follow the law, regardless of their personal views.

- **Respect the personal values of families.** This point is not in contradiction with the previous statement. Respect does not mean doing everything that families want. In the vignette, the teacher respected the father's values by listening to his perspective. In this way, a level of mutual trust could be established that allowed all parties to continue the conversation.

- **Dialogue without imposing personal values.** The teacher in the vignette may not have understood in his core where the father was coming from, but he did not impose his personal values. The conversation happened over several meetings. The father's values were juxtaposed with the ethical responsibility of educating the child in a way that is developmentally appropriate. The teacher was confident in his skills and in his knowledge of early childhood education.

- **Use the NAEYC Code of Ethical Conduct to guide your work.**

CHAPTER 3:
CURRICULUM

Advancing Equity in Early Childhood Education (NAEYC 2019)

Recommendations for Everyone: 1, 2, 4

Recommendations for Early Childhood Educators:

- Create a Caring, Equitable Community of Engaged Learners: 1, 2, 4, 5, 6, 8, 9, 10

- Observe, Document, and Assess Children's Learning and Development: 1

In the past, this Head Start program held special cultural diversity events separate from its regular curriculum. This fall, the teachers and the director decided to implement a cultural diversity goal for the entire year. That meant there needed to be evidence that the cultural diversity that children bring into the classroom was well integrated in the curriculum. The idea was that children's prior knowledge and personal interests would be used in conversations, activities, and learning about curriculum topics. It would recognize that each child brings a unique perspective. With that in mind, teachers designed curriculum for the next area of study: transportation. They wanted the children to explore transportation with a diversity perspective. They discussed the ways they go to school (school bus, parents' car, city bus, bicycle). Some children talked about how their relatives in their home country transported themselves. Other children explored the modes of transportation their grandparents used in the past. Over the course of four weeks, children shared their experiences and learned new ideas together from each other and the teachers. Since six children were dual-language learners, the teachers found the words for bus, car, and road in each of their home languages. They added them to the word wall. This honored the home languages of the children and increased everybody's intercultural understanding. They engaged the families by asking them to talk about transportation with the children at home. All of these strategies contributed to meeting the cultural diversity goal. It happened every day in a natural and organic way.

Examining Curriculum with a Diversity-Rich and Equity Lens

Honoring culture in the curriculum is more than including cultural traditions. The curriculum must give opportunities for children and adults to see themselves in it. Picking up on the vignette's topic of transportation, we can imagine that "transportation" can go from impersonal vocabulary and concepts (bus, driver, bicycle, road, truck) to personal vocabulary and concepts (*I* take the bus with *my mom* and *we* say hi to *our* bus driver; *my grandpa* rides a bicycle in his Guatemalan village; in the old days there were no roads in Somalia, *my ancestors* rode camels in the desert; *my uncle* is a truck driver, and *his* truck is big and red). Children are naturally egocentric, so this curriculum method allows them to make a personal connection to learning. They cocreate the curriculum with the adults, which increases their curiosity. It opens their minds to learning more.

Important Considerations for Educators

- To be effective, curriculum must be relevant to the learners first. Then as the children make the personal connection, they can ask more questions. If children do not have questions, the educators have the job of enlarging the children's thinking with developmentally appropriate challenges. The idea is to offer opportunities that are neither too easy nor too hard.

- Any topic or area of study is an opportunity for intercultural education since everyone will come at it from different points of view. Children, educators, and families all have ideas and questions from a personal and from a cultural perspective. You will accomplish that by using the children's prior knowledge and personal interests as the basis for the curriculum.

- Honor the languages of all the children and adults in the classroom or other child care settings.

Practical Applications

Strategies for Providing a Diversity-Rich Curriculum

- Use the K-W-L format to lead large-group and small-group discussions: what we *Know*, what we *Want* to know, and what we have *Learned*. This involves the children in learning. It honors their background knowledge and stimulates their curiosity.

- Integrate the curriculum so activities, concepts, and materials are used in all the learning centers: art, blocks, library, dramatic play, large muscle. For example, during the study of transportation, you can add small trucks and cars to the block center to use on roads and bridges made of blocks and make paper and pencils available in the dramatic play center to write addresses and maps.

- Provide repetition so children can learn new ideas in depth and practice over a period of time.

- Teach English explicitly so the children learn vocabulary and concepts they will need in kindergarten.

- Support the children's home languages by naming key vocabulary words in those languages. It is not necessary to be fluent in all the languages. It is doable to learn five to six key words.

CHAPTER 4:
PHYSICAL SPACE

Advancing Equity in Early Childhood Education (NAEYC 2019)

Recommendations for Everyone: 1, 2, 4

Recommendations for Early Childhood Educators:

- Create a Caring, Equitable Community of Engaged Learners: 1, 2, 4, 5, 6, 8, 9, 10

- Observe, Document, and Assess Children's Learning and Development: 1

The pre-K classroom had fourteen boys and four girls. Ms. Caroline, the lead teacher, believed in gender-neutral education: offer the children the same activities and they will all make the best of it. However, she felt overwhelmed with the high energy level of the boys. The girls were doing fine. They took part in the activities she planned. They listened to the stories and spent a lot of time at the art center. But several boys had taken over the room. They would build towers and knock them down loudly. They would poke each other at circle time. They would not sit crisscross applesauce at story time. When the class went to the playground, they would chase and tackle each other. Ms. Caroline realized that she disliked boys and their high physicality. She wondered how she could get them to focus and be safe. She worried that nobody was learning much in her classroom. Her beliefs in gender-neutral education were being tested. Then she did some research on gender preferences and big body play. She received observation and feedback from her program coach. Finally, she concluded she must redesign the learning environment to better meet the children's diversity of needs. She changed the classroom schedule, the physical setup, and the activities to engage all the children in more productive ways. She asked her coach to continue observations to assess the climate in the classroom. She facilitated conversations with the children about the uses of the room at different times of the day. They even learned the difference between "boisterous play" and "quiet play." Over time, Ms. Caroline found that children were more engaged in learning, and she was more satisfied with teaching.

Defining the Physical Environment with a Diversity-Rich and Equity Lens

The early childhood environment is often called the "third teacher." It promotes learning when it has the elements the children need, such as safety, a sense of belonging, and interesting materials to explore. In addition, the space must be uncluttered to promote calm learning. The opposite happens too. When the space is disorganized, overstimulating, and the activities are not interesting, children's learning is limited and their behavior deteriorates (Fisher et al. 2014).

Important Considerations

- According to the Office of Civil Rights (OCR), boys represent 79 percent of preschool children suspended once and 82 percent of preschool children suspended multiple times, although boys represent 54 percent of preschool enrollment (OCR 2014). These percentages go higher for boys of color. At the same time, most early childhood teachers are women, like Ms. Caroline, and they have to find ways to adapt to gender differences in physicality and provide equitable options to all children.

- The physical space belongs to the children and the early educators to cocreate. When children build parts of their environment, they are more engaged and contribute to their own learning. In turn that results in fewer discipline challenges. For example, in some classrooms the space must be tidied up at cleanup time, but children are allowed to keep block structures they have started over a period of days. This practice allows children to feel ownership over their work and think more deeply about their projects.

Practical Applications

Strategies for Providing a Diversity-Rich Physical Environment

- Post the drawings and work of the children at their eye level.

- Children must see themselves in the environment to feel like they belong. They should see their creations (paintings or scribbles) and their own images.

- Have mirrors so children can see themselves.

- Take pictures and videos of children jumping or running and write a story.

- Tour the environment with the list of children in your hand. Ask yourself how each child uses it. This may change from time to time, depending on who the children are.

- Establish areas for quiet play and others for active play. Talk about it with the children. Label the areas together, and discuss rules of appropriate behavior.

- Children must feel calm and not overstimulated. There should not be harsh lighting or loud music. Lights and sounds must complement the children's voices and movements, not overwhelm them.

- Have different physical options for the same activity. For example, children can paint standing up at an easel or sitting on a chair at a table. They may read on their tummies in the library area rug or sit on a couch.

- Offer a variety of large-muscle opportunities outdoors for climbing, crawling, and jumping, as well as quiet activities like sitting and chatting with a friend.

- Make the sensory table available every day so children always have the choice of sensory exploration that is calming and satisfying.

- Cocreate the dramatic play center with the children. Rather than providing a ready-made dramatic play center, propose to the children that they build it with you. Any basic furniture from a housekeeping play area can be transformed with cardboard, paper, tape, markers, and stickers. The dramatic play may follow a prescribed curriculum, or it may be developed out of an emergent curriculum format. It can be a castle, a zoo, a flower shop, a laboratory, or a rocket ship. The children contribute to it based on their individual interests. They design, build, write signage, or organize the cash register. They gain pride in their collective work. They are agents in their own learning.

CHAPTER 5: MATERIALS, BOOKS, AND TOYS

Advancing Equity in Early Childhood Education (NAEYC 2019)

Recommendations for Everyone: 1, 2, 4

Recommendations for Early Childhood Educators:

- Create a Caring, Equitable Community of Engaged Learners: 1, 2, 4, 5, 6, 8, 9, 10

- Observe, Document, and Assess Children's Learning and Development: 1

Ms. Rosie received a grant to purchase toys and books for her family child care home. Fresh from a training on creating diversity-rich environments, she browsed the catalog and found just what she needed for her multicultural group of children. She bought a multiracial set of dolls and a set of books that depicted various family constellations. When the toys and books arrived, she excitedly put them on the shelves. To her disappointment, she soon heard two children arguing about the dolls, one saying she didn't want the black doll "because she's bad." Ms. Rosie didn't know what to say at first, but she decided it was a teachable moment for her as well as for the children. The next day, she took the dolls and introduced them at circle time. The group talked about each doll. She asked the children what they thought of them. She facilitated a conversation about who they thought was "good" or "bad" and why they felt that way. Over time, they continued to discuss the value of all people. They read books with positive characters from all cultures. Since she started the discussion, her little group of children has been learning to address bias.

Examining Materials, Books, and Toys with a Diversity-Rich and Equity Lens

Materials need to mirror diversity without being stereotypical. This includes books, music, foods, dolls, wall decorations, and dramatic play props. They must show openness in gender roles, racial and cultural backgrounds, capabilities, family lifestyles, economic groups, and types of work. Some commercially available materials reinforce stereotypical views of diversity, such as pink and blue toys and posters of children from around the world in traditional costumes. These should be avoided. As Ms. Rosie learned in the vignette, educators have a special responsibility to select materials with a diversity-rich and equity lens and to help children play with them.

Important Considerations

- Materials must reflect the cultures of the classroom so the children can see themselves as well as their classmates and their teachers. They also should reflect the diversity of cultures in the wider community so children learn about others.

- It is important that educators introduce the materials, books, and toys to the children while pointing to similarities and differences. This may happen as they read books with characters of different ethnic backgrounds, skin colors, or abilities. For example, when reading *Peter's Chair*, by Ezra Jack Keats, they may say, "I notice that Peter's skin is black. In our classroom, Jamar and Lisa and Mohamed have black skin too. Just like Peter."

- As they observe children play, educators should be alert to what the children are saying. That gives them the opportunity to find teachable moments to help children think about diversity. They may hear children say they do not want to play with the doll in the wheelchair because it is "weird." Then they find the time to talk about it at the moment or at group time: "This doll needs a wheelchair to move. Some people in real life cannot walk and use wheelchairs too. In our class, nobody has a wheelchair. Do we know someone who does?"

Practical Applications

Strategies for Materials, Books, and Toys in a Diversity-Rich Environment

- Introduce books and toys. Use them to talk about differences and similarities between people. Discuss the children's feelings about differences.

- Address the children's comments and introduce them to anti-bias ideas.

- Avoid ready-made art projects. Encourage children to use their imaginations and personal styles for all projects.

- Display the children's work and talk about how they use a variety of colors and shapes in their art and thinking.

- Have toys that reflect the cultures of the children. It may be dolls with varied skin colors, flags of the different home countries of children, or dress-up clothing with items from different occupations.

- Have toys that introduce diverse perspectives to all children. For example, the dollhouse has figures of varied ages and abilities. Figures may be young or elderly, with full or limited mobility, walking or using wheelchairs or walkers.

- In the library area, feature books that reflect the family constellations of the children in the room; books should reflect the diversity of life even when the composition of the classroom appears homogeneous.

- In the art area, make available crayons and papers of different tones; have a variety of textures and colors that may be used in contemporary and traditional crafts found in the children's and your communities.

- In the block and construction area, supply a variety of transportation vehicles such as trucks, cars, motorcycles, and bicycles; supplement blocks with natural materials such as twigs or stones; feature animals that are related to the topics the children are exploring.

- In the science area, include examples and pictures that are related to the local plant and wildlife and others that are related to the place(s) of origin of the children's families.

- In the house area, feature dolls that are multiracial; include child-size or toy disability aids, multicultural foods, and dress-up clothes that represent different occupations and cultures.

CHAPTER 6: LANGUAGE AND COMMUNICATION

Advancing Equity in Early Childhood Education (NAEYC 2019)

Recommendations for Early Childhood Educators:

- Create a Caring, Equitable Community of Engaged Learners: 1, 2, 3, 7, 10

- Observe, Document, and Assess Children's Learning and Development: 1

Ms. Julie is concerned that this year she has a super diverse classroom. In her group of eighteen children, seven are dual-language learners who speak four different languages at home: Tagalog, Spanish, Somali, and Hmong. This group includes children who are Asian, Latinx, and African. The other eleven children are monolingual English speakers. They include children who are white and African American. Cultures and languages coexist in early childhood programs and can make educators' jobs challenging. The school district offered a training on teaching dual-language learners for all educators in the school readiness program. It was succinct and practical, so many questions were answered and everyone felt less anxious. They were given ten recommendations: (1) be friendly and calm; (2) speak English with confidence, clearly and slowly; (3) use gestures to complement language such as giving directions to wash hands or clean up; (4) learn comfort words for children who feel out of place; (5) read books in small groups, giving more time to look at pictures for the English learners and more time to talk for the English speakers; (6) have an integrated curriculum with activities and toys that relate to a main topic for three to four weeks in a row; (7) ask the families what they want their children to learn at school and at home, and keep these ideas in mind in planning curriculum; (8) honor the home languages by asking families to teach educators the names of the children, greetings, and songs in the home languages; (9) use the greetings and songs at circle time on a predict-able schedule to create a multilingual community of learners; 10) maintain routines to help children anticipate what's coming next and minimize confu-sion. The list gave Ms. Julie a plan to follow. It reassured her that she had good skills to tackle the year.

Examining Language and Communication with a Diversity-Rich and Equity Lens

Early educators agree with the concept of maintaining home languages in addition to teaching English. They have discarded the harsh practices of the past, such as forbidding chil-dren to speak their home languages. Yet they do not have simple answers to the complexity of teaching children in super diverse classrooms with multiple cultures and languages. From birth, children of immigrant families live in a multilingual world, with the home and dominant cultures intersecting. Educators have the job of teaching English, but they are not sure if they should teach it explicitly. They want to honor home languages, but they are not sure how. Overall, they are nervous about doing the right thing.

Important Considerations

- Educators cannot be proficient in all the languages in their classrooms. English is the language of instruction in most programs. It is the only language common to all the children together. The most practical model of care and instruction of young children is English language teaching combined with home language support. Children need to learn English skills to be successful in kindergarten. They also deserve to receive support for their home language.

- Honoring home languages means giving them a special place in your curriculum, such as the recommendation to Ms. Julie to explicitly sing songs and give greetings in home languages on a predictable routine. Honoring home languages is important in the class-room. It teaches all children that all languages have value. Monolingual English children and immigrant children learn that their friends' home languages have different sounds and words.

- Immigrant parents have faced many challenges to arrive in the United States. Their main motivation is to give a better life to their children. They want their children to maintain their home language while also learning English. Educators can support families by reas-suring them that speaking the home language at home is important. It helps families preserve their culture and emotional connections. Families also need reassurance that you will teach English in your classroom so their children can be ready for kindergarten in the United States.

Practical Applications

Strategies for Language and Communication in a Diversity-Rich Environment

- Gather information from families on the children's experiences with home languages and with English. A personal meeting is more effective than a questionnaire, especially if families have a low level of formal education or if their language is not a written language.

- Explain to parents that continuing the home language at home is good for the children and the family. It is a way to maintain a close relationship. Being bilingual is good for the brain. Children are smarter when they have two words in their head for objects and ideas.

- Translate the jargon of early childhood education into plain English when you talk or write to families. For example, "social skills" is about learning to share and getting along.

- Let families know the topic or theme you are teaching in the classroom. Give them a weekly sheet (in plain English) with the topic and the main words the children are learning. If you do not know the words in the home languages, ask a person who speaks the home language to translate the vocabulary words.

- Ask families to talk about the same topic to their children in their home languages. For example, if you are studying butterflies, children can hear about butterflies in English in your classroom. They also hear about butterflies in the language of home. That reinforces the learning of concepts.

- Have books in the languages of the children. It proves to children that their language is valued. Even if you do not know the language, you may be able to invite a parent or community volunteer to read the book.

- Schedule parents or community members to visit on a regular basis to read, sing, or tell stories in their home languages.

- Use the technique of Preview-View-Review. This technique works well to increase comprehension when you're reading a book, when you have an adult who speaks the language of the children. Preview: preview the book in the home language. Give the title and a brief summary of the plot. View: read the book in English. Review: discuss the book in the home language.

- Plan regular days and times in the schedule to honor home languages.

- During large-group time, include greetings, songs, and fingerplays in children's home languages, adding them to your English repertoire.

- Home language support does not have to be daily. However, it is best when it is planned on a predictable schedule. For example, you can make Wednesday your international day when greetings are done in the different languages of the classroom or when special visitors come to read.

- Conduct small groups in English and in home languages if you have adults who can lead them. Tell the same stories or play the same games in all the groups.

- Find short videos online to show children how to count or say the alphabet in the many languages of your classroom. All children benefit from hearing how the same activities can happen with different sounds.

CHAPTER 7:
BEHAVIOR GUIDANCE

> **Advancing Equity in Early Childhood Education (NAEYC 2019)**
>
> Recommendations for Early Childhood Educators:
>
> - Create a Caring, Equitable Community of Engaged Learners: 1, 2, 3, 7, 10
>
> - Observe, Document, and Assess Children's Learning and Development: 1

Anthony was a four-year-old African American boy. Every day at cleanup time, Anthony would jump on a table. His teacher, Ms. Angie, would tell him with a smile: "Anthony, could you please come down?" But typically, he looked at her and yelled, "No!" Sometimes she tried to get him down physically but he would resist. Other times she ignored him, and he would eventually get down on his own, though he still wandered through cleanup. It was a frustrating trial and error situation. In contrast, Anthony generally cooperated by putting on his coat before going outside. On the playground, he ran around and played well with the other children. But when it was time to go in, he would stop cooperating again. Even when Ms. Angie coaxed him with, "Could you please come inside to have snack?" Anthony looked at her and said, "No!" Ms. Angie's words were patient, but her body was stiff. She had had enough of the boy's negative behavior. She had already sent him out to the director's office several times, just to get a break from him. She was beginning to think he should be assessed for special education. Fortunately, Ms. Angie had the support of a coach who observed her classroom regularly. The program philosophy was not just to "observe the children" but to observe the entire environment: the space, curriculum, instruction, activities, teacher-child interactions, and transitions. The observation revealed that a predictable pattern had developed in the interaction between Anthony and his teacher around transitions. She tried to be nice, but her irritation was obvious. He seemed to understand the rules, but he was being asked to make choices he didn't want to make. In consultation with the coach, Ms. Angie designed a three-prong strategy: (1) Have a conversation with Anthony five minutes before cleanup time to talk about the expectation to put toys away and not jump on the table; (2) At the beginning of cleanup, say in a firm voice with a serious tone, "Anthony, remember, no jumping on the table today. It's time to pick up toys. Here is a truck. Put it on the shelf now."; (3) Affirm Anthony when he cooperates: "Anthony, thank you for putting the truck on the shelf. You are a good helper." Within a week, the problem was solved. Both Anthony's and Ms. Angie's confidence in their skills increased. And they were well on the way to developing a positive relationship.

Examining Behavior Guidance with a Diversity-Rich and Equity Lens

Behavior guidance is the aspect of early education that is most vulnerable to educators' biases. Focus on providing behavior guidance rather than classroom management. Classroom management is about control and punishment. Behavior guidance is about teaching young children the social skills they need to function in the social setting of the classroom. Children must learn self-awareness, self-control, cooperation, and empathy. Punishment teaches criticism, confrontation, humiliation, and retribution (Gartrell 2004).

Important Considerations

- African American boys like Anthony are disproportionally assessed for disabilities. They often get a vague diagnosis of an emotional or behavior disorder for defiant attitude. They are also expulsed from early childhood programs at an alarming rate (Gilliam et al. 2016; OCR 2014). Teachers tend to attribute reasoning beyond their developmental age. This results in teachers not knowing how to guide behavior in positive ways. With good intention but few strategies, they believe that the only solution is special education.

- When early educators have preconceived ideas about children's behavior based on gender, race, ethnicity, or socioeconomic status, they expect that children will exhibit negative behaviors, such as interpreting wiggly children as disruptive. In their eyes, these children are not merely learning social skills appropriate to their level of development. They are more likely to want to fix these children to fit their vision of the perfect child.

- Be aware of your biases against all children, especially boys, children of color, and children in poverty. Train yourself to look at these children with a positive lens (Sullivan 2016).

Practical Applications

Strategies for Behavior Guidance in a Diversity-Rich Environment

- Use appropriate body language and words for the situation.

- When children are cooperating and following directions, smile and give affirmations that describe what they are doing well individually or as a group: "Wonderful, Jamar, you have been patiently waiting for your turn!" "All children, I noticed how you all worked together to clean the room. That was good cooperation!"

- When children are not cooperating or following directions, use a direct tone and a serious expression: "It is not OK to be on the table. You need to get down from the table right now."

- Be straightforward. Children rely on visual cues to understand their world. A teacher sends a confusing message when she appears to be smiling but is obviously irritated.

- For children who are dual-language learners, use English for directions or discipline. Children understand if you say clearly and with gestures: "It is time to wash hands. You wash hands at the sink. I will show you."

- If children have done something inappropriate and need correction, speak in English and use gestures as necessary: "Everybody sit down now. Sit on the rug." When teachers use the home language mostly to get children to comply, they send a disrespectful message. It tells the children that the home language is only good for management.

- Make a firm rule that a person's identity is never a reason to tease or reject them.

- Be aware of the language you use with your colleagues to describe children's behaviors. Words like *aggressive*, *at risk*, and *unteachable* promote a negative climate.

- Be aware of the language you use to describe your day. Words like *crazy*, *climbing the wall*, and *insane* promote a negative climate too.

- Use language that promotes a positive climate: *enthusiastic*, *high-energy*, *engaged.*

CHAPTER 8:
FAMILIES

Advancing Equity in Early Childhood Education (NAEYC 2019)

Recommendations for Early Childhood Educators:

- Create a Caring, Equitable Community of Engaged Learners: 1, 5

- Establish Reciprocal Relationships with Families: 1, 2, 3, 4, 5

While dropping off Kevin (three and a half years), his mother told teacher Maria that the night before nobody slept. The family had a big party to celebrate the arrival of a cousin from Florida. During the day, it was obvious that Kevin was tired. He whined, grabbed toys from the other children, and was generally in a bad mood. Maria was irritated at first. She blamed the little boy's behavior on the excitement of the big party. She felt his mother was irresponsible in letting him stay up on a weekday. This had happened before. In the past, teacher Maria was very judgmental. This time, she caught herself. The month before, the center offered a parent workshop on the importance of sleep. Kevin's sleep pattern improved after his mom attended. Last night was a special occasion. So, Maria treated this situation as special. At lunch, she talked with Kevin about the party. He said it was fun. Teacher Maria told him that he needed to rest at naptime. She stayed with him a few extra minutes until he settled down. When Kevin's mom picked him up, Maria reported on the not-so-good morning and the better afternoon. The mom smiled and said she remembered the workshop on sleep and that tonight her son was going back to the early bedtime routine. Teacher Maria smiled too. Her goal of establishing reciprocal relationships with the families of her children was happening.

Examining Families with a Diversity-Rich and Equity Lens

When we work with children, we work with families too. Some educators find that challenging. They say they have more patience with the children than with their parents. Understanding behaviors of adults can be more complex, especially if they are different from your expectations.

Important Considerations

- Families may make decisions in ways that differ from how you, the educator, would respond. In some families, men and women may make decisions based on their skills, religious beliefs, or roles assigned by their culture. The family is the ultimate decision-maker for services and supports for children.

- At the same time, the educator's job is to prepare parents to make informed decisions. We are cultural guides to education. Educators have formal training and experience that families do not have. It is the job of educators to guide all families to understand our work of educating their children.

- All families want to be welcomed. The early education environment can be intimidating. Parents have fears and hopes for their children, and they want reassurance that their children are well taken care of. They have important funds of knowledge about their culture and their children. Yet immigrant families who were successful in raising children in their home culture may be bewildered by the host culture where they are now.

- Educators must be open and curious about what the families expect. That helps them be culturally sensitive. Families are curious about teachers too. They want to know who this person is who spends so much time with their child.

Practical Applications

Strategies for Supporting Families in a Diversity-Rich Environment

- Listen to the perspective of families by giving them opportunities to say what they think. Do this in person during a conversation. Written questionnaires are intimidating. Not all parents have the level of literacy to feel comfortable answering.

- Share about yourself, your culture, your family, and your education. This sets up an important personal connection with the children and their families and builds your relationship.

- Explain to families how your learning activities help educate children. Describe your curriculum. Make the connection between the activities and the skills the children need to learn according to early learning standards. For example, if your topic is birds, they can talk with their children about birds at home too. This is helpful for families who are English speakers and for immigrant families who are learning English.

- Use plain English. Clarify the jargon we use in early childhood education. Rather than talking about *cognitive development*, define what it is with examples such as *how children learn and think, make decisions, and solve problems*. This is useful for all families. It is necessary when you work with an interpreter for immigrant families.

- For written materials, translate the jargon first into plain English. When jargon is translated directly, it is impossible to understand. This is intimidating for families, who may feel inadequate when they cannot follow.

- Offer reassuring messages that you and the family are working together to teach their children.

- Ask for family contributions for all your topics or areas of study, not just for folkloric celebrations. Families do not want to have their culture on display. They want to be cocontributors to the community of your classroom or center.

- Have a no-fault attitude with families. They all want their children to succeed in school, academically and socially. But parents do not have the same background in education that educators do. They cannot be blamed for not knowing as much. Educators must give them tips to help their children learn at home. These could range from tips for toilet training to literacy tips, such as telling stories or finding letters of the alphabet on the cereal box.

- Give families feedback on how their children are learning in your program. Make the connection between what they are learning and how they are preparing for the next step, such as moving to the toddler group or going to kindergarten.

- It is OK to tell families they are their child's first teacher, but it is a problem to expect them to teach early literacy or math when they do not have the skills. Make the distinction that educators are the "teachers for school" and families are "the teachers for life."

CHAPTER 9:
COLLEAGUES

Advancing Equity in Early Childhood Education (NAEYC 2019)

Recommendations for Everyone: 1, 2

Recommendations for Administrators: 6

Happy Children Child Care center served sixty children in seven classrooms. The director and three lead teachers had college degrees. Four teachers had a CDA. They ranged in age between twenty-two and fifty-nine. The director and two teachers were white, three were African American, and two were Asian. The teaching assistants were Latina and white. All were women. Everyone appeared friendly and caring. There was a sense that the staff liked working with young children. At the same time, the relationships between colleagues were strained. A lot of gossip happened behind the scenes. Several times a day, staff members were found whispering in the hallways, sometimes in their home language, making mean hand signals or refusing to cooperate on classroom duties. Gossip was rampant, and the director was concerned. Finally, she organized a workshop for all staff. They learned that gossip is contrary to the goal of developing healthy social-emotional skills for children. The colleagues realized that they were contributing a negative model of diversity, pretending to get along but sabotaging each other daily. After heartfelt discussion, they all decided to change the culture of their center. They made a pact to stop gossip and use the parallel process: treat each other as they strive to treat children.

Examining Colleagues with a Diversity-Rich and Equity Lens

Early childhood education is an entry field to the workplace for many immigrants and new workers, especially women. Even with low levels of education, it is easy to get jobs as classroom assistants and aides. It is important to reflect on how personal backgrounds might affect communication and relationships. NAEYC's Code of Ethical Conduct has a section on coworkers:

> Principle I-3A.1—To establish and maintain relationships of respect, trust, confidentiality, collaboration, and cooperation with coworkers. (2011, 5)

This principle fits with the goals and practices of anti-bias, pluralism, cultural guidance, and skilled dialogue in chapter 1. It is a parallel process to what we expect early educators to do with children and families. They need to apply the same standards to interactions with each other.

Important Considerations

The unifying goal in our field is for all children to receive high-quality early education. This goal is being accomplished by a diverse workforce that has needs for recognition and support. Good educators create a caring community of learners with their children. They also strive to create a caring community of colleagues that respects differences.

The social environment of a center contributes to a sense of safety. Child care centers and schools are workplaces where intimate stories are shared often. This sharing may be necessary so teachers know how to better care for children. Staff often share their own personal stories too. In relationship-based environments, gossip becomes an occupational hazard.

Practical Applications

Strategies for Working in a Diversity-Rich Environment

- Gossip creates a negative climate. It must be addressed and stopped. The most effective strategy is to address the problem directly as in the vignette. One particular exercise used in workshops is to ask a volunteer to squeeze toothpaste out of a tube. Then ask them to put the toothpaste back in, which obviously cannot be done. It is a visual example of how hurtful words once spoken cannot be taken back.

- If you or a coworker have concerns about a colleague's behavior, even if children's well-being is not at risk, these concerns should be addressed. For example, there may be differences of style in how educators interact with children. Some teachers use indirect language such as, "Will you put on your coat so we can go outside?" Other teachers use direct language: "Put

---

your coat on. It's time to go outside." Often these differences follow cultural preferences. Educators may judge each other to be too lenient or too harsh. Through talking about the situations and listening with empathy, you can understand each other better and value the benefit of each approach.

- Licensing rules, best practices, and program goals are nonnegotiable professional responsibilities. They occasionally may conflict with personal cultural beliefs. Maintain ongoing dialogue with colleagues to sort through your feelings and find solutions that work.

- Create a caring community of workers by smiling, greeting each other, and sharing materials and equipment.

- Attend professional development on the topics of personal disposition and learning styles. Colleagues report relief when they find out who the extroverts and the introverts are on their team. They realize the differences in reaction are not mean-spirited or strange but rather are just personality traits.

- Attend professional development on the topic of cross-cultural competence. Many behaviors can be logically explained by understanding one another's cultural practices.

- Intentionally follow up after each professional development session. Write a goal that you want to implement and post it in a place where everyone will be reminded of it. For example, one team made the goal to find teachable moments to talk about race with children, such as when reading books. Though it felt a bit awkward at first for some teachers, it soon became a positive practice that benefited their diverse student body.

- Learn about each other through small informal interactions that build cohesion and interest in each other, such as sharing desserts at staff meetings or sharing a favorite game from your own childhood.

- Recognize that we all have biases, based on our life experiences and personal stories. Be vigilant about your own biases. Implicit biases are hard to detect. For example, educators with a high level of formal education may not trust that parents with a low level of education know what their children need to learn. When parents ask the teacher if their child is learning the ABCs, the teacher may dismiss the question and talk about the child's behavior, saying the alphabet is not as important as sitting quietly in school. This situation is likely to lead to conflict. Parents with low formal education have high hopes that their children will succeed academically. They want their child to do better in school than they did themselves. Therefore, their main questions will be about learning to read, write, and do math. These matters are not as important to well-educated teachers, who by definition have been academically successful themselves. In this case, keeping in check the implicit bias that the parent is an ignorant person who should know better, the teacher would respond first to the academic questions and explain clearly how they teach the ABCs and how the child is learning them. If behavior was indeed a barrier to learning, then the teacher could explain how the parent could help the child change behavior to learn the ABCs better. This measured process (based on the skilled dialogue approach) would allow the parents's concerns to be validated. It would fulfil the recommendation of Advancing Equity to "establish reciprocal relationships with families" (NAEYC 2019, p. 8).

CHAPTER 10:
PROGRAM LEADERSHIP

Advancing Equity in Early Childhood Education (NAEYC 2019)

Recommendations for Administrators: 2, 3

Recommendations for those Facilitating Educator Preparation: 1

Located in a rural area, the Head Start program had a large population of new immigrants who worked in food canning plants. One-third of the children were dual-language learners. Finding staff that reflected the diversity of families was challenging. The program hired seven foreign-born employees with no experience in early childhood education, limited English language skills, and unknown home language skills. They were assigned the title of cultural navigator but did not receive any training for their jobs. These cultural navigators had cultural sensitivity for children and families of their own culture, but they did not have the professional skills to function in the program. There were a couple of unsatisfactory years, during which the navigators did not understand their responsibilities and other staff was getting frustrated. Finally with the help of a consultant, administrators, teachers, and navigators created a job description with a defined role in the classroom and home visits. The cultural navigators received special training in child development and early childhood education. The classrooms received books and materials in the languages of the children. The cultural navigators were encouraged to attend free English classes for adults. They proudly advanced in their bilingual skills and their roles. The quality of the program steadily improved for all children and staff as the new educators became more competent and confident. In this case, the program leaders focused resources to scaffold the professional learning of the cultural navigators. They accomplished the goal of creating a diversity-rich environment with an equity lens.

Examining Program Leadership with a Diversity-Rich and Equity Lens

The NAEYC guiding principles for educating children must be matched with parallel guiding principles for education leaders. In my book *Evaluating and Supporting Early Childhood Teachers*, I make the case for education leaders to support teachers in the same way that they expect teachers to care for and educate children (Passe 2015). The idea is to create a caring community of workers, enhance professional competence, provide appropriate direction and resources, assess professional skills and growth, and facilitate involvement in the field of early childhood education. These five principles serve the cause of creating a diversity-rich environment for staff.

Important Considerations

Leading and growing a diversity-rich environment is complex work. Education leaders have to pay attention to the needs of the children, families, and staff. Leaders must be alert to set the tone for comfort and openness. They have the responsibility to facilitate the variations in communication styles caused by the interactions among many cultural dimensions. A young parent's informal style may clash with the formal style of an experienced teacher.

Education leaders also have to manage for educational quality. As in the vignette, new staff members have the potential to be an invaluable addition to the quality of the program, but many steps have to be put in place to make success happen. It is a priority to hire employees who reflect the diversity of the families and children. However, it can be challenging to implement given the skill sets required by licensing and other regulations. To achieve the goal of diversity and equity for all, extra time and money may be necessary for professional development, coaching, and supervision.

Practical Application

Strategies for Leading the Creation of a Diversity-Rich Environment with an Equity Lens

- Hire employees who reflect the diversity of children and families.

- Talk about cultural differences and similarities in daily conversations.

- Share ideas and beliefs from your own culture. Accepting that everyone's culture has value is the first step. It contributes to open communication.

- Facilitate discussions about cultural differences and similarities in ideas about raising and caring for children.

- Listen to staff cultural perspectives related to the job of caring and educating children and working with families.

- Compare staff ideas about caring for children with the expectations related to licensing and best practices. Find common ground.

- Provide differentiated professional development opportunities. All staff must have the skills to care for and teach the children. However, given the differences in background, they do not all need to sit in the same professional development workshop.

- Communicate in several ways (group meetings, individual meetings, email, text message) to address the varied styles and abilities of staff.

- Celebrate success by recognizing the positive elements of your work: the learning of children, the appreciation of families, and the friendships of staff members.

- Use a tool to self-assess your program. The Diversity-Rich Environment Checklist at the end of this book is intended as an overview of practices that respect and promote cultural and linguistic diversity. It is a tool for self-assessment and discussion, not an evaluation instrument. As you use it in your program, you will get a sense of the areas where you are strong and where you can improve.

CONCLUSION

Putting It All Together: Creating a Diversity-Rich Environment for All Children, Families, and Staff

It is critical to stop overt cultural bias or prejudice. This is the most important discussion that any staff needs to have. Implicit bias is not always easy to spot, however. It may hide behind good intentions. For example, in some programs, children who arrive late, during circle time, are not allowed to join the other children on the rug. Instead, they are directed to a table to eat a late breakfast. The educator's bias is that children need to eat before they can learn. While they have their breakfast away from the group, they miss story reading and all the other things taught at that time. The result is that the children's learning is compromised. It can also lead to behavior problems as these children are not integrated into the community of learners already sitting on the rug. Other programs use an approach that meets the need for learning and the need for food in a different order: the children who are late are welcomed directly into the circle where they can participate immediately. They listen to the story and get all the benefits of learning in large group. At the end of circle, they have the option to eat breakfast for a few minutes at a small table in the room. The second scenario results in children who are more engaged in the activities of the classroom. Their learning is enhanced. In this case, the educator prioritizes teaching (her first responsibility) while understanding that the children must eat. As you are making policies in your program, consider how you can maximize opportunities for children's learning.

When educators know about families' stresses, such as poverty, they are more likely to have low expectations of children's behaviors and ability to learn. On one hand, they excuse negative behavior, blaming it on the challenges of the family. On the other hand, they teach less and lower the quality of the curriculum. They may focus on providing mittens and food rather than intellectually engaging learning activities. That sets a negative cycle for the children who are then understimulated.

It is important to have discussions about how best practices in the field of early childhood education dovetail with cultural expressions. Some of the directives in our field are health and safety requirements for all children. Others are standards for teaching and learning. As you develop and implement curriculum, talk about how the best interests of the children are served from the two angles: cultural sensitivity and best practices in early education.

Creating diversity-rich environments is more than a promising idea—it is both reparation for the past and investment in the future. Reparations are called for because we have made biased mistakes that have hurt children in the past, but now we know more than we did then. Early educators cannot claim ignorance about the value of educating all children. The infamous achievement gap begins in the preschool years. The stakes are high for social-emotional learning as well for academic learning. Children develop their self-awareness as good people and their self-confidence as capable people in our environments. All the suggestions in this book aim to give you strategies to expand your view of diversity and to continue to improve your important work.

"All Children Deserve the Opportunity to Reach Their Full Potential" (NAEYC 2019, p. 16)

In the language of resilience research, educators are a protective factor. Despite the other circumstances in children's lives, your classroom, center, or family child care home is the place where children can thrive. You are the professional for the job. You can introduce children to the diversity of their country and the world with books, stories, videos, and your own example. You have the gift of offering children a positive view of themselves and each other. This immense privilege is entrusted to early educators every day by families, community, and ultimately the nation.

At the Transforming Challenging Behavior Conference (May 8, 2018), Megan Pamela Ruth Madison said, "I am not responsible to complete the work, but I also don't have the choice to opt out." It seems like the perfect motto for this endeavor of creating diversity-rich environments for young children. The idea is to take small, steady steps in the right direction of creating a caring intercultural community in classrooms and family child care homes and in our centers or programs. There may be moments of discouragement. Challenges may not be resolved easily. But it is essential to stay the course.

APPENDIX: DIVERSITY-RICH ENVIRONMENTS CHECKLIST

This checklist is intended as an overview of early childhood and family education practices that create diversity-rich environments. It is a tool for self-assessment and discussion, not an evaluation instrument. All the items are important. Check the appropriate box on a scale of 1 (lowest) to 3 (highest).

In our program:	1 No	2 Kind of	3 Yes
Values and Attitudes			
Educators share collective understanding about the dimensions of diversity			
Educators learn from families the ways that family members help their children succeed			
Educators are sensitive to families' needs and requests			
Educators reinforce the core values shared by families in program			
Educators understand how families teach resiliency (spiritual values, executive function)			
Educators explain to families the best practices in education that they use in the classroom			

Educators guide families to learn about the culture of the field of education			
Educators understand that family's reactions and approaches (e.g., to health, discipline, disability, diet, self-help) may be culturally based			
Educators problem solve ways to educate and support all families, with the awareness that some family members may have biases			
Educators learn from each other the ways that they use to have children succeed			
Educators discuss their own biases regularly and problem solve the best ways to educate and support all families in their program			
Communication with Children and Family Members			
Educators communicate with families about children's development using the early learning standards of their state as a guide			
Communication assistance is provided for parents who need it (e.g., language interpreter, plain English, extra time to communicate)			
Written communication is adapted to families' literacy levels and is supplemented with oral communication (e.g., flyer and phone or in person)			
Educators learn and use greetings and comfort words in the children's home languages			
Educators do not use children's home language for discipline			
Visual props and gestures are used to augment the message and increase comprehension for children and families			
Educators teach English with intentionality, using developmentally appropriate best practices			

Educators know that not speaking English well is not a limitation of mental ability			
Educators know that having a low level of formal education is not a limitation of mental ability			
Curriculum and Teaching			
Educators teach all children the skills they need for school success according to the Early Learning Standards			
Teaching is differentiated so each child learns the skills			
Educators recognize each child's strengths and interests in the curriculum			
Teaching is a balance of child- and adult-led activities			
Active learning happens daily through play and exploration			
The curriculum is integrated across areas of knowledge and development			
Diversity is not just for special times—it is part of the daily curriculum			
Educators support the maintenance of home languages at home and at school			
Educators teach English intentionally at school			
Families are regularly invited to participate in sharing their practices, languages, and traditions relevant to the curriculum, not just for folkloric events			
Classroom visitors (readers, expert community workers, family members) are diverse (ethnicity, occupation, gender, ability)			
Educators use children's biased comments as teachable moments			

Behavior Guidance			
Educators are aware of personal biases when interpreting behavior of children			
Educators provide a predictable environment with routines			
Educators plan and design spaces for active play throughout the day			
Educators plan and design spaces for quiet play throughout the day			
Educators calmly explain the rules of the environment, using repetition and gestures			
Educators give affirmations for positive behaviors, not making automatic "good job" statements			
Educators use direct tone and serious expressions for corrections or management			
Educators do not use home language for corrections or management			
Educators use positive language to describe behavior of children to colleagues			
Environment and Materials			
The environment and materials reflect the diversity of the children, families, and educators: toys, photographs, illustrations, posters, props			
Materials and books do not reinforce stereotypes			
Books are in English and the languages of the children, families, and educators			
Books have stories and information relevant to children's everyday lives			
Music reflects the diversity of families and educators			

Meals include some foods familiar to children			
Families regularly share their stories and cultural traditions			
Educators regularly share their own stories and cultural traditions			
Program Leadership			
Program leaders intentionally hire staff (teachers, administrators, paraprofessionals) to reflect the diversity of families and children			
Program leaders understand and explain the importance of creating a diversity-rich environment for all children, families, and staff			
Program leaders provide necessary resources for materials and books to create a diversity-rich environment			
The professional development of all educators and administrators includes cultural and linguistic competence			
Program leaders provide guidance and support for all educators though performance evaluation			
Program leaders provide ongoing professional development and coaching to maintain a diversity-rich environment			
Program leaders continually assess the quality of their diversity-rich environments			

RESOURCES

Sources for Books and Materials

AMAZEworks (www.amazeworks.org)
AMAZEworks is an organization that provides training, coaching, and materials to promote anti-bias education in early childhood.

Cooperative Children's Book Center (CCBC) (https://ccbc.education.wisc.edu)
The CCBC is part of the University of Wisconsin-Madison School of Education. It has extensive lists of multicultural children's books with reviews and links to more resources.

Just Us Books (http://justusbooks.com)
Just Us Books is a publisher of Black-interest books for children. The books reflect the diversity of Black history, heritage, and experiences.

Mantralingua (www.mantralingua.com)
Mantralingua is an online bookstore that sells children's books and games in fifty-two languages. Its goals are to provide resources for minority languages around the world and to celebrate the cultural and linguistic nature of society.

Milet (www.milet.com)
Milet is a multilingual publisher that has titles in twenty-six languages. Milet publishes an extensive collection of dictionaries on CD, as well as other materials for children and adults.

Multilingual Books (www.multilingualbooks.com)
Multilingual Books is an online bookstore offering children's books in one hundred languages. Most are bilingual with English. Well-known favorites, such as *Brown Bear, Brown Bear, What Do You See?* and *Goldilocks and the Three Bears*, are available in languages such as Urdu, Tamil, and Arabic. The website also offers DVDs, CDs, and software for children and adults.

Social Justice Books (https://socialjusticebooks.org)
Social Justice Books is a project of Teaching for Change. It identifies and promotes lists of
   books on the topics of equality and diversity. It has extensive reviews by experts.

Websites

Colorín Colorado (www.colorincolorado.org)
Colorín Colorado is a bilingual website (in English and Spanish) for families and educators of
   English-language learners. It is an educational initiative of public television station WETA
   of Washington, DC, in collaboration with the American Federation of Teachers, the National
   Institute for Literacy, and the U.S. Department of Education. Its free, web-based service
   provides research information, activities, and practical advice for educators and Spanish-
   speaking families of English-language learners.

Early Childhood Learning and Knowledge Center (http://eclkc.ohs.acf.hhs.gov)
This website is a service of the Office of Head Start. It offers information and tips for parents,
   teachers, and administrators on all aspects of early childhood. The Office of Head Start
   includes the National Center for Cultural and Linguistic Responsiveness, and the website
   includes a section dedicated to dual-language learners and their families. The "Program
   Preparedness Checklist" is available here. This checklist helps programs assess whether
   their systems, policies, and procedures meet the needs of children and families who speak
   languages other than English. It provides useful information for program planning and
   professional development.

FPG Child Development Institute (www.fpg.unc.edu)
The FPG Child Development Institute, formerly called the Franklin Porter Graham Center, is
   part of the University of North Carolina at Chapel Hill. It is a multidisciplinary organization
   that studies young children and their families. More than two hundred researchers,
   students, and staff work on projects dealing with parent and family support; early care
   and education; child health and development; early identification and intervention; equity,
   access, and inclusion; and early childhood policy. In addition, FPG publishes curricula,
   resource guides, reports, and articles.

National Association for Bilingual Education (NABE) (www.nabe.org)
NABE represents both bilingual learners and bilingual education professionals. Its five
   thousand members include educators, researchers, policy makers, and parents in twenty
   states. Its mission is to advocate for bilingual learners and their families and to promote
   native-language as well as English proficiency. The association works toward intercultural
   understanding and respect.

National Association for the Education of Young Children (NAEYC) (www.naeyc.org)
NAEYC is a member organization with local, state, and regional affiliates. Its mission is
   to improve the well-being of all children from birth to eight years old by improving
   the quality of early childhood programs, teachers, and caregivers through adherence
   to developmentally appropriate practice. The organization sponsors and produces
   professional development conferences and educational materials, including position
   statements on major issues such as the teaching and assessment of dual-language
   learners.

National Black Child Development Institute (NBCDI) (www.nbcdi.org)
NBCDI focuses on the well-being and early education of Black children zero to eight years,
   with a cultural competence lens. It serves as a national resource agency, supplying
   programs, publications, advocacy, and training.

National Center for Cultural Competence (http://nccc.georgetown.edu)
The National Center for Cultural Competence is in the Center for Child and Human
   Development at Georgetown University. It provides training, technical assistance, and
   consultation; contributes to knowledge through publications and research; creates tools
   and resources to support health and mental health care providers and systems; and
   supports leaders to promote and sustain cultural and linguistic competency.

National Center for Learning Disabilities (www.ncld.org)
The National Center for Learning Disabilities provides information and promotes research on
   effective learning. It addresses the needs of dual-language learners.

Plain Language (www.plainlanguage.gov)
This website was created by the Plain Language Action and Information Network (PLAIN), a
   group of federal employees who support the use of clear communication in government
   writing. They develop and maintain the content of this site. It has information on the Plain
   Writing Act of 2010, and many resources to keep writing clear and free of jargon.

U.S. Citizenship and Immigration Services (USCIS) (www.uscis.gov)
USCIS is the government agency that oversees lawful immigration to the United States. Its
   website provides a wealth of information to help you understand issues that immigrant
   families may be dealing with.

U.S. Department of State (www.state.gov)
The U.S. Department of State provides up-to-date information on the languages, people,
   geography, history, economy, and politics of countries around the world.

WIDA: World-Class Instructional Design and Assessment (https://wida.wisc.edu)
This website presents a system of thinking about English-language learners developed at the
University of Wisconsin. WIDA's philosophy is that children need to develop strong skills
in academic language to succeed in school. The WIDA teaching and assessment system
addresses both social language and academic language.

BIBLIOGRAPHY

Barrera, Isaura, and Robert M. Corso. 2003. *Skilled Dialogue: Strategies for Responding to Cultural Diversity in Early Childhood.* Baltimore, MD: Paul H. Brookes.

Barrera, Isaura, and Lucinda Kramer. 2017. *Skilled Dialogue: Authentic Communication and Collaboration Across Diverse Perspectives.* Bloomington, IN: Balboa.

Bell, Kim. 2019. "The Sunshine Call: Celebrating Children's Successes." *Teaching Young Children* (12) 3.

Bowman, Barbara, ed. 2002. *Love to Read: Essays in Developing and Enhancing Early Literacy Skills of African American Children.* Washington, DC: National Black Child Development Institute.

Bowman, Barbara. 1999. "Kindergarten Practices with Children from Low-Income Families." In *The Transition to Kindergarten*, edited by Robert C. Pianta and Martha J. Cox, 281–304. Baltimore, MD: Paul H. Brookes.

Brown, Katie E., and Aimy S. L. Steele. 2015. "Racial Discipline Disproportionality in Montessori and Traditional Public Schools: A Comparative Study Using the Relative Rate Index." *Journal of Montessori Research* (1) 1.

Delpit, Lisa. 2006. *Other People's Children: Cultural Conflict in the Classroom.* New York: New Press.

Derman-Sparks, Louise, Maria Gutierrez, and Carol Brunson. 2009. *Teaching Young Children to Resist Bias: What Parents Can Do.* Washington, DC: NAEYC.

Derman-Sparks, Louise, Debbie LeeKeenan, and John Nimmo. 2015. *Leading Anti-Bias Early Childhood Programs: A Guide for Change.* New York: Teachers College Press and Washington, DC: NAEYC.

Derman-Sparks, Louise, and Patricia G. Ramsey. 2011. *What If All the Kids Are White? Anti-Bias Multicultural Education with Young Children and Families.* New York: Teachers College Press.

Fisher, Anna V., Karrie E. Godwin, and Howard Seltman. 2014. "Visual Environment, Attention Allocation, and Learning in Young Children." *Psychological Science* 25 (7): 1362–70. https://doi.org/10.1177/0956797614533801.

Gartrell, Dan. 2004. *The Power of Guidance: Teaching Social-Emotional Skills in Early Childhood Classrooms.* New York: Delmar Learning and Washington, DC: NAEYC.

Gilliam, Walter S., Angela N. Maupin, Chin R. Reyes, Maria Accavitti, and Frederick Shic. 2016. *Do Early Educators' Implicit Biases Regarding Sex and Race Relate to Behavior Expectations and Recommendations of Preschool Expulsions and Suspensions?* A research study brief. Yale University Child Study Center. https://medicine.yale.edu/childstudy/zigler/publications/Preschool%20Implicit%20Bias%20Policy%20Brief_final_9_26_276766_5379_v1.pdf.

Gonzalez-Mena, Janet. 2008. *Diversity in Early Care and Education: Honoring Differences.* 5th ed. Boston: McGraw-Hill.

Howard, Tyrone C. 2019. "Capitalizing on Culture: Engaging Young Learners in Diverse Classrooms." In *Spotlight on Young Children. Equity and Diversity*, edited by Cristina Gillanders and Rosella Procopio, 31–44. Washington, DC: NAEYC.

Huber, Mike. 2017. *Embracing Rough-and-Tumble Play: Teaching with the Body in Mind.* St. Paul, MN: Redleaf Press.

Masten, Ann. S. 2014. *Ordinary Magic: Resilience in Development.* New York: Guilford Press.

NAEYC (National Association for the Education of Young Children). 2011. "NAEYC Code of Ethical Conduct and Statement of Commitment." *NAEYC.* naeyc.org/sites/default/files/globally-shared/downloads/PDFs/resources/position-statements/Ethics%20Position%20Statement2011_09202013update.pdf.

———. 2019. "Advancing Equity in Early Childhood Education: Position Statement." *NAEYC.* www.naeyc.org/sites/default/files/globally-shared/downloads/PDFs/resources/position-statements/naeycadvancingequitypositionstatement.pdf.

OCR (US Department of Education Office for Civil Rights). 2014. *Civil Rights Data Collection: Data Snapshot: School Discipline.* Issue Brief No. 1. www2.ed.gov/about/offices/list/ocr/docs/crdc-discipline-snapshot.pdf.

Oliva-Olson, Carola, Linda M. Espinosa, Whit Hayslip, and Elizabeth S. Magruder. 2019. "Many Languages, One Classroom: Supporting Children in Superdiverse Settings." *Teaching Young Children* 12 (2).

Passe, Angèle Sancho. 2013. *Dual-Language Learners, Birth to Age 8: Strategies for Teaching English*. St. Paul, MN: Redleaf Press.

———. 2015. *Evaluating and Supporting Early Childhood Teachers*. St. Paul, MN: Redleaf Press.

Shareef, Intisar, and Janet Gonzalez-Mena. 2008. *Practice in Building Bridges: Companion Resource for Diversity in Early Care and Education*. 5th ed. Washington, DC: NAEYC.

Sullivan, Deborah Ren-Etta. 2016. *Cultivating the Genius of Black Children: Strategies to Close the Achievement Gap in the Early Years*. St. Paul, MN: Redleaf Press.

Wright, Brian L. 2019. "Black Boys Matter. Cultivating Their Identity, Agency, and Voice." *Teaching Young Children* 12 (3).

Printed in the USA
CPSIA information can be obtained
at www.ICGtesting.com
JSHW062345230424
61790JS00003B/4

9 781605 546650